Where There Is Love...
We Are One

by **MARIAN S. TAYLOR**

Illustrations by Amy Duarte

Balboa Press books may be ordered through booksellers or by contacting:

Balboa Press
A Division of Hay House
1663 Liberty Drive
Bloomington, IN 47403
www.balboapress.com
844-682-1282

Because of the dynamic nature of the Internet, any web addresses or links contained in this book may have changed since publication and may no longer be valid. The views expressed in this work are solely those of the author and do not necessarily reflect the views of the publisher, and the publisher hereby disclaims any responsibility for them.

ISBN: 978-1-9822-1082-3 (sc)
ISBN: 978-1-9822-1081-6 (e)

Library of Congress Control Number: 2018909999

Print information available on the last page.

Balboa Press rev. date: 08/19/2021

Interior Graphics/Art Credit: Amy Duarte

BALBOA.PRESS
A DIVISION OF HAY HOUSE

Where There Is Love....
We Are One...

As a little child, I come to earth
to fill many hearts with love.

I am excited to share my love and smiles,
so below as it is above.

As I get bounced from Dad to Mom
and back again to Dad.

I feel such comfort, love, and joy.
There is no room for sad.

This love is comfortable and special and true.
It's something I don't have to learn.

I feel it in each hug, each smile.
I feel perfect love at every turn.

We each begin life with love in our hearts, and each holds love for those close to them.

There is love for a parent, a sibling, a child... there is love for relatives and friends.

There are friends from other countries
who hug and caress their loved ones dear.

There are families playing and giggling together.
Love is the same there as it is here.

Some friends live in houses
that are high above the sea,

But they still eat and sleep
and love their families.

Some friends wear different kinds
of clothes than I wear,

But they still play and pray
and love and share.

Some cover their heads,
some bow, and some kneel.

It's all a sign of respect
and how they feel...

For you Holy One, shining down from above...

We feel your peace... your peace and your love.

No matter the way we eat, dress, or pray...

It's about how we show love each moment of each day.

I know the Love of Heaven so well...

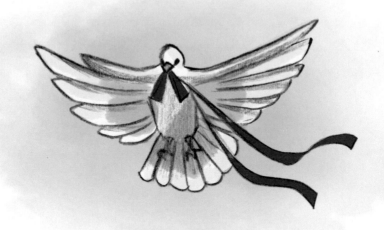

This is the Love I've come to tell.

About the Author

    Marian S. Taylor, EdD, is a retired university professor. Her career began at the elementary level where she taught first grade and served as a reading specialist. She was director of the university laboratory school and a chairperson of a university department. She taught undergraduate and graduate classes while at the university and spent many years directing the program for the development of reading specialists.

    Marian has been very involved with her family and with church activities. She is the mother of three grown children and is very proud of her grandchildren.

www.marianstaylor.com

About the Illustrator

    Amy Duarte began her career as an artist working for Walt Disney Animaton Studios. From there, she leapt into the world of visual effects and graphic arts on more than 30 feature films like "*Pirates of the Caribbean: At World's End*," "*The Amazing Spiderman*," "*Mr. and Mrs. Smith*," etc. She was appointed as a lead artist for several major motion pictures, including "*Fantastic Four*," where she advised and guided a team of artists on creating the special effects of Jessica Alba's character (Sue Storm).

    Born in Jakarta, Indonesia, and raised in three different countries, Amy is fluent in six languages and an avid polo player. She was also on the design team that created the top secret commercial for Apple's Watch before the product was lauched. Her portfolio can be viewed at:

www.amyduarte.com

Printed in the United States
by Baker & Taylor Publisher Services